Seven Miles Deep

Seven Miles Deep

Pamela Garvey

Five Oaks Press
FIVE-OAKS-PRESS.COM

Copyright ©2017 Pamela Garvey
All rights reserved. First print edition.

Five Oaks Press
Newburgh, NY 12550
five-oaks-press.com
editor@five-oaks-press.com

ISBN: 978-1-944355-23-4

Cover Art: Victoria Rich
www.victoriarich.com
Cover and Book Design: Stacey Balkun

Printed in the United States of America

ACKNOWLEDGMENTS

Bad Shoe: "Abra Cadabra"
Cimarron Review: "Of Which She Said Nothing" as "Blue Jays"
Contemporary Verse 2: "After Her Son Disappeared" as "Interview with a Mother Plaza de Mayo, Argentina"
Cutthroat: "Prayer's Equation"
New Millennium Writings: "Chosen" as "Dogs"
Pleiades: "Persephone's Autumn Farewell"
Rhino: "Seven Miles Deep" in an earlier version titled "Trembling" (second place in 2009 Editors' Choice Awards)
Smartish Pace: "The Desaparecido's Confession" as "Interview with a Desaparecido, Argentina" (finalist for 2007 Erskine J. Poetry Prize)
Sonora Review: "El Mozote"
Southern Indiana Review: "In the Light Provided by the Baltimore News" & "After the Massacre" as "Fear"
Sou'wester: "Wasps" & "Two Figures"
Superstition Review: "The Dark, a Child Listening" & "Pain Tolerance"
Talking River Review: "These States"
UCity Review: "Among Fish Without Eyes"
Valparaiso Poetry Review: "The Wasp Nest Growing Inside Our Window Pane"

The following poems were published in a limited edition chapbook entitled *Fear*, from Finishing Line Press (2008):

"Of Which She Said Nothing" as "Blue Jays"
"The Tide" as "The Waves"
"The Annunciation"
"Chosen" as "Dogs"
"Virgins and Mothers"
"The Desaparecido's Confession" as "Interview with a Desaparecido, Argentina"
"These States"
"El Mozote"
"After Her Son Disappeared" as "Interview with a Mother of Plaza de Mayo, Argentina"

"Insomnia"
"After the Massacre" as "Fear"

The following poems were published in a chapbook entitled *Things Impossible to Swallow,* from 2River Press (2013):

"The Dark, A Child Listening"
"In the Light Provided by the Baltimore News"
"Cocaine"
"Swollen" as "Under Yellow Jackets"
"The Distant"
"My Brief Stint as an Infested Angel" as "St. Jude's Nursing
    Home"
"Serious To Do List"
"Elbowed"
"Things Impossible to Swallow"

The author thanks the following people for their support, encouragement and assistance with poems in this manuscript: Barbara Perry, Patrick Donnelly, Martha Rhodes, Joan Houlihan, Allison Funk, Richard Long, Ellen Bryant Voigt for everything she taught me, and most importantly Andrew Miller for his countless and invaluable critiques of the individual poems and the manuscript as a whole.

For Isaac

"*If you've never wept and want to, have a child.*"

--from "Incarnations of Burned Children" David Foster Wallace

CONTENTS

Wasps   7

I.
Of Which She Said Nothing   11
The Tide   12
The Annunciation   13
Gifts I Adore   14
Inaugural Scene   15
She Who Can Sleep in a Horse's Stall Nose to Shit   16
Cocaine   17
The Men Who Steal Her from Her Mother   18
My Brief Stint as an Infested Angel   19
What I Wanted   20
What Philomela Wants   21
In the Light Provided by the Baltimore News   22

II.
Wasp Eyes   25
The Dark, a Child Listening   26
The Distant   27
Chosen   28
Virgins and Mothers   29
El Mozote   30
These States   31
The Desaparecido's Confession   32
After Her Son Disappeared   33
After the Massacre   34

III.
Insomnia   37
Swollen   38
The Wife's Lament   39
Reading the Lover's Palm   40
All that Was Felt and Never Said   41
Things Impossible to Swallow   42
Elbowed   43
Serious To Do List   44

My Love Life in Less than One Hundred Words	45
Marriage	46
The Wasp Nest Growing Inside Our Window Frame	47

IV.

Void	51
Persephone's Autumn Farewell	52
Prayer's Equation	53
Abra Cadabra	54
Among Fish Without Eyes	55
Witch Child	56
Pain Tolerance	58
The Cello, Leaving	59
If There Were a God, and If That God Had Eyes	60
Family Portrait with Birds	61
Parable of the Blind	63
Dead Nests	64
Seven Miles Deep	65
Notes	69

Wasps

paralyze spiders with a single
sting. The still bodies
they drag to rotten

and half chewed joists
deep in the porch. Here
their eggs hatch into

a writhing grave.
To lie undead like that spider,
everything frozen but

fears clicking through
the brain. I have been
buried in such a sleep.

I.

Of Which She Said Nothing

                      Bald, wings striped
silver and blue, skin yellow
as the feet through budding tufts, wings
twisted in, bones snapped.
                      One chick alive—
eye open toward a sky of
birch leaves and a woman squatting
and peering—opens and closes
his beak as if only hungry as
flies arrive and head for belly
and chest.
                      If my mother were here,
she'd choose a stone or spade head—flat,
accurate. I once touched a warm,
blue body, too young to see what
she insisted was right. Peering
through blinds, I saw her lift the spade.
She said nothing after. If only
I'd vowed to own no such tools.

The Tide

When she twirls, her skirt
spins into a saucer. The grass
dizzying around her shins.
From nowhere, boys charge, chase her into
the cement culvert that leads to the sea. Didn't she
see them waiting? Hadn't she been warned
about boys? Couldn't she foresee
the ground slick with wet leaves,
dog piss, spilled oil? She hopes
for their sympathy. Somehow slides, falls
foolish, into the leaves. Rises at the laughter
cornering, pulling her down again
by the hem of her skirt. Their faces
blur: one grins another's teeth;
one's eyes under another's brow.
Even their voices, one voice.
Like waves, like the distant,
regardless tide.

The Annunciation

Don't believe what they've told you; the angel
spoke not a word.
       Just a thrashing, an invisible
thrashing around me. A gust
shook me awake, kicked sand through
       the paneless window and across
my face. A tug at the blanket, then
at the sleeve. My hair blowing into my eyes,
       I stood up, tensed when a thing like
silk or oil slid along my neck.
He siphoned the air.
       But my clothes weren't even
roughed, my skin not bruised. I would've been
grateful for such evidence.
       But it's the nature of couriers
to be quick.
Before I knew it, the seed
       tumbled within. Released, I turned,
as if he had a face, as if he
could be pointed to in a line of men.

Gifts I Adore

My mother aims a ladle at my face,
asking *Why? Why?*
Is that me tying a string of Kens together
to heel behind my roughed up doll?
That woman, that mother,
turns her head from sorry lies.
Why destroy gifts I adore?
Like a man does
when he crosses a woman he loves.
Who tears off her dress
and burns it at the stove?
Who grabs a meat cleaver
to sever hair?
Who gouges paint from plastic eyes
with scissors? It's harder work
than you'd imagine—all this punishing. And
for what? A man
who works late, leaves a woman
staring at a plate of food
she later flings?

Inaugural Scene

I hear it. Like a baseball bat beating
the underside of a sheepskin rug,
then a whimpering—faint, waning. Being a child,
I know all those sounds. Still, I pull apart
the plastic slats in the fence just to see
the fist, the crouching into the dirt.

She Who Can Sleep in a Horse's Stall, Nose to Shit

trembles for a fix, breaks the gate off the hinges, gags
at the sight of her mother's biscuits with honey. She
smears horseshit in doorjambs, flings the mother's panties

around the house for cops to finger and smell. She
never confesses. She stages it as crazy thieves. Sells
the mother's jewelry, curls up next to piles

of shit, lets the wind swallow that mother's voice
begging *come back where all is okay, all
is* . . . Nothing's okay when the pipe's empty.

Cocaine

hummingbird pulse
feeder taps its morse code into
the awning   window blazing
with spikes of sunrise   pupils
like wasp eyes   winged things
under the skin   needle cuts
the same niche in the record
over and over   sweat spots
shirt, pants, the bed
trembles   a few drinks to torch
the ice of consequence

The Men who Steal Her from her Mother

Some acid tripping Jesus with flask and
pistol, bitch seat primed
for her, inner shins burned on the exhaust.

Some whiskey stealing Sinatra flitting
thumbs through flames, flicking
halos of gnats from her ankles.

Some dope peddling professor of
anatomy, some side swiping salesman of time
shares, some bookoo rich bookie blasting

the horn for her to come
to him. And this girl who's always
too cool to run, hustles out the door

because she knows when he wraps his arm
around her shoulder, he's the kind who'd shoot
a horse between the eyes to win a bet.

My Brief Stint as an Infested Angel

I steal. From the stash for the wheelchair flock.
At first just one Valium. At first
just from patients already half-baked
and dressed in bed sores. Now I steal
from those wailing in Alzheimer's. I swallow fistfuls
of Martha's meds. I let Martha shove
spoonfuls of puddings into toothless mouths.
I let her crumble bread she'd otherwise spit
into potted plants. I steal
the plants and blood pressure gauges and slippers
that don't fit. I steal light bulbs
and mop heads and cram them in my closet. I steal
moans that wake me from Vicodin sleep.
I hide them under my pillow, wake
to them every evening, don the puppy dog scrubs
I stole. I steal the call buttons,
ripping wires right from walls.
I clutch the frayed ends, fling them at mirrors.
Arthur calls me sweetie; Mary, in her smoker's rasp
yells *Sugar, Sugar come to me.* Richard cradles my face
in his palsied hands. He calls the necklace I stole a halo.

What I Wanted

    In response to Francis Bacon's painting *Two Figures*

Are their eyes open? What
does the one man clench with his teeth—
rag or rope—as the other straddles
him, pins him down? Is
that man pinning him down?
Brushstrokes seem to shimmy
on this unprimed canvas, the rough side
the painter always chose. I, too, wanted the raw
untreated surface.
So everything would soak in:
another's sweat, another's weight grinding
the body, so high I forgot I lived in it.
The arms—they seem to flail. Like my past,
nothing in this painting is still
even though everything is still.

What Philomela Wants

Those damn Romans change every story they steal.
As if I'd trade places with my singing

sister, beak and chest stretched almost to tearing.
You think I still need to grieve, prefer that

to the swallow's appetite? I fly into
a sky where human eyes can't even spot

insects I scoop mid-flight, mid-dip, gliding
and hunting flickers—so much more paltry

than the boy who begged for nothing because he
trusted us. Who'd believe a mother

would choose sister over son? Myth makers—
what do they know of her mourning in trills

while I soar, feathers the color of steel,
wingtips like blades. My flight—sharp turned stabs.

In the Light Provided by the Baltimore News

Outside wind sifts snow to the ground,
half burying whatever people drop—
bottles, receipts, photo of a boy and a woman
crouching with a dog. In the bar's dull light,
he speaks almost in whispers, muffled
by a TV news flash
of a man who snapped, killed wife
and kids. I've barely begun
to work again. I drink vodka neat, try
to learn new languages in preparation
for some big move, something important I can't
quite name, so I make up stories
about a Brazil that doesn't exist,
a job as a correspondent, as if
the man cares. Back at my place, Don—
that is his name, that
is what he tells me, or
what I remember—Don, in his whiskey voice, asks me
if I ever thought about killing anyone,
my face in his hands, his mouth moving over mine.

II.

Wasp Eyes

The compound eye—one
hundred eyes without a lid
to shut out the light.

The Dark, a Child Listening

night after night, eyes prowling
the sky outside for the death regatta
rowing in the distance. I hear

the oars splashing, the churning depths.

Stars barnacle the keels of their fleet.

My mind hurries to ready itself
for those pale throngs.
How long? How soon?

I can't stand the way day is bruised
with darkness, how the owl-clock
cocks its plastic eyes,

points lopsided wings at glowing numbers.

The Distant

Who created God? Did Mary spank Jesus?
And why did soldiers shoot

at you? "I hid in the birch leaves," she replied,
"buried myself in piles.

They walked right over me. That's how I got
this." She poked lumps on her knee,

crooked, broken bone never set. She sang
to me of County Kerry's

valley of the birch, of rebels martyred by
soldiers. To distract me

from the doctor wrapping my wrist in plaster. I
caught sight then in her eyes

of holy wells reflecting birch's blue.
She stares out the window

all day now. Knee still bruised, my wrist long healed.
Rosaries dropped to her skirt's well.

Old Woman, do your prayers sink to muck? Do
soldiers still colonize

memory? With what hands have you strength enough
to slap the face of Christ?

Soon you'll lie again beneath birch leaves, the boots
pressing down on you—mine.

Chosen

Biblical, my mother insists, the flea infested
scrawny ribs chosen for me
after someone tossed her to the streets
and she followed me home. In my mother's world
dreams of horses promise money
on the way. An itchy right ear means the town
is talking highly of her deeds. This dog means
good luck. It's as if I could walk safely through minefields.
All her sniffing and twitching of ears and nostrils
to herd me through fields. My mother lifts my hand—
oil and dander stuck under the nails—
and kisses the tips of my fingers
as if they belonged to a saint.

Virgins and Mothers

What did the Virgin know when she palmed
                            the soft spot of the baby's head?
Anything? Not the sting
                            of a crown of thorns?
A wasp nest balloons from the eaves,
                            the virgin workers
hunting too close
                            to the crook of my son's elbow.
Wasps do not hum,
                            they do not buzz. They are
too close to my son's crib. I must destroy
                            the nest, all the young, always
defended by needles so small I can't even see them.
                            These virgins don't bleed
enough. Can a woman be broken and fierce?
                            Can I? Nothing fierce in
the Mary of triptychs and statues.
                            Broken first by a baby
and not a man, not desire.
                            Sometimes, holding my son,
I can hear trembling, my own body. The poison
                            that paralyzes wasps
could linger in the nursery, cling
                            to any surface. I
must smoke them out after removing
                            all his clothes and diapers
and blankets. He is no cherub-
                            like infant promised a kingdom.
He squirms and roots for the breast.
                            When he nurses, he looks
through my eyes as if they weren't there,
                            as if he hears the future
hatching inside paper.

El Mozote

He leans against the town
water pump, the only blue thing
among miles of coffee, banana, corn.
I came back now it's safe,
he says, asking us not for running water
or electricity, but a church
to replace the collapsed
chapel where the town's men
(or did he say women?) were lined up
and shot. A dusty barefoot girl
chases us. Her mother watches
from a hollow in the clay house.
Diez colones, she says, offering
a rusty bullet the length of her palm,
and unearthed, she insists,
near the human bones. *Diez colones,*
she says. So I pay.

These States

Honey faced and hoarse, our darlings
pitch baby pumpkins like grenades,
capsize stop signs, splatter strangers' yards,
trip an alarm, then bolt skeleton-masked,
daring each other: wouldn't the alley, full
of trash cans, look better on fire? Yes, it would,
of course it would. The fruit of our loins
laughing at the nursing home's bed bound
peering at them through the fire escape.
What do our boys know about absentee ballots
like kindling amid magazines and old news
around the edges of beds? It's
election night. Low turnout, a landslide.
Sugared up with his friends, my son
swears he never meant it to happen.

The Desaparecido's Confession

I shivered. No blankets or shoes, no heat
or companion. They covered my head with bags of lime. I
    collapsed.
I lay still. The windowless walls tied me. For days,
maybe weeks, I was blindfolded. My eyes, at first,
roamed beneath. A swirl of pocketed moths.
                      My son once pocketed moths
to feel them flutter until they couldn't. I wish
I could wander the streets and stop staring into the eyes
of those I pass. So much never fits. When they touched
the electricity between my legs again, I
screamed names of people I barely remembered,
faces I wouldn't even recognize.

After Her Son Disappeared

I hover always
at the epicenter. Breathe
as if gravel

were suddenly winged.
I crawl through cracks
in earth's crust

foraging for a cradle
that squeaks, a boy
whose laugh

is diamonds. He is
my breath's arrow,
creature wild as a river.

I wish I could drown
in his rushes.
A log, loitering. A wind, less

than a whisper.

After the Massacre

Dandelions rise among bone chips of children.
Mari wakes to save someone.
She claws at the walls of a well.

What is that song children sing when they pop
the heads off dandelions? Flowers planted
near the memorial sway headless to that song.

The weight of the past drags her down.
A body tied to other bodies tied to stones
thrown into that water like a deepening bruise.

Immunity?
Histamines. Dissonance
climbing the stair of white blood cells.
Muscles constrict. Passages narrow.
What's caught in the lungs?
A trigger, her baby's cough, her boy in a ditch: clothes
stained with dirty blood? The sloughing
skin falls like snow.
St. Anthony's fire. Her body
a monument
sinking.

> One that's gritty,
> dirt filling its cracks. How easy
> to fall for the sterility of polished metal
> on display by a sign that reads "Don't Touch"
> because then we'd know how cold it is, that something
> was left out, emptied into the void
> with no surface to echo what's lost.

Children? Husbands?
She dug a hole into the maguey's ground, pressed
her mouth into dirt.

The soldiers *didn't want to*.

III.

Insomnia

undrowning   surfacing   flailing
of blankets   in the throat:
unspoken words   salt water gulped
burning   slivers of dawn   fringed with birds
starling and jays   louder than those words
unspoken   stinging   whose mouth?
covered yours?   who cried?   who
stung?   who disappeared?   the bed fails
to swallow   pray to drown   pray for underwater deaf
muffle, muzzle this mind   light years away
whose cock?   whose fist?
what did you fail to say?   wedged
in the recesses   swelling like a paper nest
each comb   a kaleidoscope
voices:

Swollen

The man, asleep on the hammock, snores and doesn't
stir at all as yellow jackets mill around his face and throat—
attracted by the crust of barbecue sauce on the chin. At first
she thinks to wake him. Instead she dreams of herself
stinging his swollen neck with peroxide.

The Wife's Lament

The eagle piping
from the top of a birch,

the mate's responding trill—
high pitched yet softened by distance
here by the river.

These sunless days there's less glare from the ice.
Days, a dog's sigh, a dog's breathing.
You've drug yourself to the river's edge
only because I begged.

From the eagle's nest, a low echoing
like a purr, impossible to locate in the perfect
camouflage of mist and bark. Where are you? January drone.
Shadows like sponges. Dusk falls,
you sleepwalk home through the opiate cold.

I wonder if you've noticed
the eagles. Have you noticed
the eagles?

Reading the Lover's Palm

This line traversing the thumb spells avalanche.

It doesn't mean I'm your destiny.

At the base above the wrist
a small v stands for voracity.

It has nothing to do with me.

You even confuse left and right. On the one
hand, solitary confinement.
On the other, the depression at the bottom
of the ring finger mirrors the cave
where you got lost.

All That Was Felt and Never Said

I never said what I needed to.
Silence sticks to cells, multiplies
its void, a virus; your name
a gasping. Each word of the unsaid

a lytic split as the host explodes,
choking on laughter, which
long ago died. Body heavy
with heat, corrupted by the noise

of words never spoken
clogging tissue, sinew, muscles
aching so I couldn't even raise
my hand to hush you. I want to lift

from the tub that fevered
young woman I was. Naked,
she hallucinated a man with your
name, shivered shut up.

Things Impossible to Swallow

Her own ecstasy when he ties her
to the bed, and she begs as the rope
wears at the skin of her wrists.

Does she really lap up every touch, every
word that sours her own laugh?

That smack she shuts inside with rising temperatures
of work, pay. Poor and no time
to read. She's become stupid, he says. And she bites
his neck harder than he likes.

Still she returns daily to the mirror he holds for her.
She breathes its mercury, leaching into veins, into
the fatty tissue that holds it in.

Herself bonded inextricably.

But someone threatens
to leave? Who? Whose head
hangs in shame? Is that her
pounding on doors, bills wound into fists?

And her, pleading:
a dog that doesn't even know when it's full.

Elbowed

Snatching stacks of bills from her hands, the man
elbows the boy. The child locks himself in

the bathroom, drinks Benadryl while they
pretend silence. The boy screams *I wish*

a semi sliced me in half, then you'd feel sorry.
With a wrench, he cracks the window; his face

in glass sparkles with cuts radiating
from the nose. A line to the ear smacks of the scar

on the father's face now under the mother's eyes.
If only he could punch through this reflection,

kick back shards, climb out without stabs or splinters.
One, a voice hollers, *two* . . . that yanking again:

cords ripped from walls. Then the slammed door. He prays
for the father to come back while the mother hugs

the dog like a favorite. When the boy
comes out, he marches over, grabs the bills

the father dropped to the floor, shreds and stuffs
them down the sink, runs faucets to flooding.

Serious To Do List

Quick drinking. Aimless
texting from alleyways. No pleas
to that asshole. No spewing hate-speech
targeting self. Valium, vespers,
voodoo dolls you'll dance
into a daze, then bury
in dirt dogs pee in. Scrub off scent—
piss scent? his scent? Black out
birthmark on his scalp, tequila bottle
tattoo, tequila-burned voice, veins
bulging, all cells still stinking
of him. Never become
the step-sister who'd slice off
her heel to fit into a glass slipper. She
gets her eyes pecked out anyway.
If you want to be blind, stuff a rocket
with every photo of self
with him. Launch it at the sun and stare
at the sky until it bursts. Prayers
of flame and fog. Amen?
Digital face turned ash—whose?
my face?—those
bloodshot eyes, that puppy dog drag.

My Love Life in Less than One Hundred Words

I debuted with suck and sacrifice

added sentimental leavening

and the buffering of a great fuck.

I graduated to hover.
Where *If* kept me lingering.

But *if*
belongs to the romance of shame, as in
if I hadn't apologized like I was begging,
begged like I was singing . . .

Behind me now:
those days when he brought lilies,
dresser crowded with bouquets.
Petals in the mirror,
the smell of facelessness.

When I fell for him
                       I felt hollow stemmed,
                       pruned.

I did not know
it was an amputation.

Marriage

Like this sculpture? At least to me, unschooled
in art. But I know about rendering
a thing splinterless. How planks hang as if
suspended mid-air, against gravity.
I, too, know something about bending boards
into arcs with tongues and grooves that don't quite
fit. Really nothing here fits. One corner
seems hollow; the other twists out like a
spring but with no flex or bounce. Stiff, yet in
motion—the coil's forward momentum
jutting out in a slimmer and slimmer
semi-circle. It's titled Off Course.

The Wasp Nest Growing Inside Our Window Frame

It's eating the air. Cell by cell,
tiered hexagons, tumorous and hollow,
cram the space between outside and in. I fog
the pane with my breath. Study all that body work:
nest from spit, warmth from wing beats. All
that fathering and only one queen. The privilege
or the price of her royalty? Which is she—
whose stinger yields offspring? Which
her nuns? Their attack always plural, arms
pocked with fires under skin. Such fierce
mothering frightens you,
muttering words like Black Flag and smoke, your lips
pursed as if ready to laugh at me
when I forbid you destroy them. I spy you
skirting hedges, shooing them away, brows furrowed
and mouth wide as if to scream. Once making love,
I opened my eyes to that same expression
as if you knew how I wanted nothing more
than to smack you. The drones—
has she finished with them yet? Have they died
and littered the yard? Why don't you sweep
them up? Why don't you count them? Why
flinch when I tap your shoulder?
Why tremble so? Why run? Why defend
with poison? Why loosen
your tie as if you can't breathe?

IV.

Void

> *The most important element of wasp and bee control is to destroy the nest.*
> --Illinois Department of Public Health

Yellow jackets nesting in a void you
cannot locate. Cheek and ear pressed against
plaster, eavesdropping on hollows. You've swollen
to almost twice your size with child, water
rising in joints. If you could chase them out
with a broom, first frost would kill them. Still the nest—
you can't leave it. Absurd to climb ladders
when you can't even bend. No way you'll plug
every seam between ceiling and wall before he—
before, simple preposition, but what
can "before" promise us other than void?

Persephone's Autumn Farewell

I am pearled in the strung light of lampposts.
Petalled ground holds me as rhododendrons
curl into fists. Pity me? No. Pity
women held by televisions, clicking in
wood paneled basements, reeking of mold. They
can be smothered instantly—tripped wires,
dropped cigarettes—smothered into this dry
rotting earth I can abandon with ease.
Only wind follows, knots rough leaves into
my hair, a flurry, flowing in westerly
gusts. You'd like to touch it, pick out crisp leaves,
smooth my tangles. You'd like to pull dried mud
from split ends as if you could just pluck his
stain from my head, with one comb rake me pure.

Prayer's Equation

The dead sparrow dumped in the compost
rots into stray feathers,
fulfilling a promise long made: X times Y times X . . .
my mother, hunched in pews
chants her pleas.

Abra Cadabra

I'll capture that mourning dove,
make it live in my room. I'll gather branches
to tie to my bed with rope.
He'll build his nest in that tree
over my pillow.
With toothpicks and fur and the rings
Daddy gave you—you won't need them
when you die. Abra cadabra: you're worms
my bird will eat.

Among Fish without Eyes

Like the blind navigating the damp down here
in the caverns. My son whispers,
turn the light back on, and then
our faces are reflected. This pool so still
it mirrors even the scar under his brow,
even the knot at the bridge of my nose.
Then fish without eyes
swarm through us. Where
do we begin? Where do we end?
Noses and eyes shimmer
into gills and tails. My lips
elongate. His limbs vanish
in thin streams. Is that him
mute and finned? He dips
his net, calls me
his prisoner.
My mouth puckers, belongs to another
saying my son's name
in a voice that frightens him.
Shuddering, he pokes a fish where eyes would
be, socket with thin fold of scales
which jerk. *Let it go*, I say. When he does,
it folds, rises, lingers on the waves
of my head. *Look, Mommy,*
you've got a white horn.

Witch Child

My boy captures me in houses
of gingerbread. With a wave of the spoon,

I'm a brother and sister
chilled to sherbert in a story of simple sugars.

My leg he bakes with dead bees
he slices and serves

wearing my old black t-shirts
and pointiest shoes—for he is Golda

who lives with mommy cats in a castle
where he locks children

from daycare in the dungeon.
Whispering, he asked brown "recklers"

in the basement not to bounce off webs
and bite him. It didn't hurt, he swore,

when mites crawled up his arm
the day he lifted a dead robin.

He called the mites flurries
of the snow queen's sleeve.

He held out his arms, closed his eyes
and said he could reach the moon on a broom.

The day comes when no one hears
a mother's hollering her child's name. I

glanced up from the park bench.
It was as if he had suddenly splintered

into the mass of children.
Only from the top of the jungle gym

did I catch him, knee-deep in leaves, bent,
laughing, witch hat pointing at the setting sun.

Hugged, he felt like bones.
Slapped, like flakes of glass.

Pain Tolerance

If a cleaver nicks a finger
chopping onions, if a splinter
of glass lodges in the heel, she sees
the crooked stream of blood
trickle over the knuckle or
toward the grouted tiles,
but feels nothing. Inside the same.
When the oncologist asks why
she didn't come sooner, she shrugs. The brain
inside a body at which a radio's
been thrown, turns the volume so low,
nerve endings only whisper.
Even years after, when a hand strokes
a back, the brain recites its mantra:
hush, hush, hush.

The Cello, Leaving

In the metro, I eavesdrop on the cello
crooning in the earphones
of the man next to me.
                      What ignites the self

to flare in multiples of four,
vivace and allegro?

Is it simple biology?

The male cardinal trilling
from a low limb
in a birch, throat stretching
to a higher octave, chest ballooning?

He calls the mate to attention: her body tipped
over a branch, hollowed.

I'd like to call the man who made me tremble
when his fingers plucked
pieces of leaves from my hair.
My mother did that years before.

I bent my neck until it stiffened
leaning toward them so they might reach and ready me
as a bride is preened white and new
for her love.

It took so long to take flight.

Why can't I remember his laugh, or even
my mother's?

Whose elbow jabs me now? Whose cologne
on my scarf? His? The cello, it sounds . . . is
one of them
leaving.

If There Were a God, and If That God had Eyes:

black holes guzzling stars, gasses, eagles

soaring with prey, dogs crouching,

mothers sliding under

morphine.

Family Portrait with Birds

While the wife sketches starlings, the husband
    aims a rifle at the tree, tracks
        the screeching.
Should cook the damn birds, he says.

Two shots echo over the jingling of the dog's tags
    as she runs to retrieve. The wife turns to
        a clean page, draws
splayed wings, eyes stuck open. Titles

it *Effigy* and promises the dead they won't
    be wasted. She *could* fashion
        bird effigies
from feet, beaks and bones, then hang one over

her son's door. She could call them *Ghost Snatchers*
    to assuage his fears. Or he'd hammer
        it up himself, stroke the toes
the same way his grandma dips fingers in holy water.

She lifts a pencil, drafts another effigy. This one she'd
    dangle from the rearview mirror—
        an apology to starlings.
A reminder to herself to keep looking back

as if what shrinks, then vanishes, behind her
    were her own humanity. She'll
        do none
of these things. She'll reward the dog

with a rawhide. She'll toss the birds into
    a compost heap. Her husband
        will teach the boy
about the Big Bang and Darwin. No

ghosts. But the boy will hold up a dream
catcher the shape of a web and say
"There's something else
you're not telling me, and I can't spell it,"

voice cracking, thinning to mere threads.

Parable of the Blind

In the museum I come upon the blind
    beggars. Riveted by doughy, diseased eyes
        Breughel studied on 16th century streets,
            I'm close enough to touch the Plague. So
                close I might set off an alarm as harsh as
                    my soon-to-be ex-husband's "What?" as he

enters the room, discovers our five-year-old—
    boy who clings, who rubs my wrist until skin
        chafes—is not by my side. Locked in the loose
            flesh of the beggars' sunken cheeks, I shake
                my head no before turning away from this
                    painting. My husband's hands seem giant

empty of our son's grip. "Not with you?" I ask.
    "What?" Guards speak into walkie-talkies; they
        bar every exit. Darting through rooms, calling
            our child, we crash into each other, knocking
                each other into door frames, hands grasping
                    at the other's waist, arms, shirt, face—for

balance or direction I don't know—but just as
    the beggars—one down, the next tumbling to
        the fallen lying in a stream—we couldn't see
            fields and churches all around us. Years, we
                dammed our own stream into which we finally
                    tripped. Does it matter who stumbled first?

Absence: a walking stick lifted off the ground
    onto the shoulders of another. Can't steady
        oneself after the partner falls. This man in
            the painting, walking behind his cohort with
                buckling knees, no wonder his mouth is stuck
                    open in an agony for which no words exist.

Dead Nests

Wasps' combs, their history of
a queen
tunneling through paper, now

dust and collapsing
old lungs.

Where do I begin?
When I open my mouth,
I come to an end. Of self?

Is that the promise?

Fire? Lashings of wings
beating too quickly to see?

Their holes,
I cannot leave them alone.

I want to strike a match
to what remains.

Seven Miles Deep

I.

I shot a girl, my friend says after I ask
what he learned at war. I am clipping lilies

for his grave. He tells me there is no love
to redden the pine and blue the birch.

With a heaving breath from the Gulf, he
recedes into starlings calling in the fog.

II.

I shot a girl, my friend says after I ask
what he saw at war. I see

his eyes and lips looming behind
Halloween masks of heroes and monsters.

Speaking as if he just rose from the ocean,
my friend tells me what my son will do

dressed like a wolf, like a ghoul, like a sniper
clutching that rifle, waiting, trembling.

III.

I shot a girl, my friend says after I ask
who he killed in the war.

*She stood by a well, held in her hand
a glistening bundle that turned somehow*

into a nest of wasps: the compound eye—
one hundred eyes without a lid to shut.

*If I could close the lids, redden trees, hide
and stop the blare of spotlights . . .*

*She was just a child I mistook
for a boy with a field pack.*

IV.

I shot a girl, my friend says after I ask
how he has come home. *She had*

your son's face, he explains,
which I have stolen back from her.

*She had your son's cries, which I bring
back via the barracks of your dreams.*

His apparition gray as scales, everything
but his voice muted as if I'd slipped

under water and his words were my pulse.
The child she carried in her arms, he is here

*beside you: nest of wasps studying
your trembling sleep.*

V.

I shot a girl, my friend says after I ask
how. At my heels petals disappear,

and I can hear, *didn't want to,*
so the Major seized a little boy,

threw him in the air and impaled him.
There is a place in the ocean seven miles deep

where fish without eyes had never seen, never
felt, the light. So scientists sent cameras down

to film them, flailing.
This is the light I hold to my son,

to my dead. What boy could forget?
I must carry him, this field pack, away

from the well, up from the depths
of this sleep and toward dawn's bluing birch.

Notes

Final line of "El Mozote": colones are Salvadoran coins

"After the Massacre" & "Seven Miles Deep": "the soldiers didn't want, so the major seized a little boy, threw him in the air and impaled him" is from Mark Danner's *The Massacre at El Mozote*.

www.ingramcontent.com/pod-product-compliance
Lightning Source LLC
Chambersburg PA
CBHW071754080526
44588CB00013B/2237